Dear Parent:
Your child's love of reading starts here!

Every child learns to read in a different way and at his or her own speed. Some go back and forth between reading levels and read favorite books again and again. Others read through each level in order. You can help your young reader improve and become more confident by encouraging his or her own interests and abilities. From books your child reads with you to the first books he or she reads alone, there are I Can Read Books for every stage of reading:

SHARED READING
Basic language, word repetition, and whimsical illustrations, ideal for sharing with your emergent reader

BEGINNING READING
Short sentences, familiar words, and simple concepts for children eager to read on their own

READING WITH HELP
Engaging stories, longer sentences, and language play for developing readers

READING ALONE
Complex plots, challenging vocabulary, and high-interest topics for the independent reader

ADVANCED READING
Short paragraphs, chapters, and exciting themes for the perfect bridge to chapter books

I Can Read Books have introduced children to the joy of reading since 1957. Featuring award-winning authors and illustrators and a fabulous cast of beloved characters, I Can Read Books set the standard for beginning readers.

A lifetime of discovery begins with the magical words **"I Can Read!"**

Visit www.icanread.com for information
on enriching your child's reading experience.

Paddington's Prize Picture. Text copyright © 2017 by Michael Bond. Adapted from the original story written by Michael Bond. Illustrations copyright © 2017 by HarperCollins Publishers. All rights reserved. Manufactured in China. No part of this book may be used or reproduced in any manner whatsoever without written permission except in the case of brief quotations embodied in critical articles and reviews. For information address HarperCollins Children's Books, a division of HarperCollins Publishers, 195 Broadway, New York, NY 10007.
www.icanread.com

Library of Congress Control Number: 2016949907
ISBN 978-0-06-243077-9 (trade bdg.) — ISBN 978-0-06-243076-2 (pbk.)

Typography by Brenda E. Angelilli

17 18 19 20 21 SCP   10 9 8 7 6 5 4 3 2 1   ❖   First Edition

PADDINGTON'S
Prize Picture

Michael Bond
illustrated by R. W. Alley

HARPER
An Imprint of HarperCollinsPublishers

One morning, Mrs. Brown
sent Paddington to the market
to buy some oranges.

Paddington was well-known
in the market.
The traders always saved
their best fruit for him.
And he always thanked them for it!

When he was done shopping,
Paddington visited
his friend Mr. Gruber.

Mr. Gruber's store was filled
with old things,
but he always had something
new to show Paddington.

Mr. Gruber was very busy.

He was washing a painting.

On one half Paddington saw

a picture of a boat.

On the other half Paddington saw
what looked like a hat.

"Just you wait," said Mr. Gruber.

"There's more to come."

"I've never seen a picture
like this before," said Paddington.
"That's because one picture
is hidden under another,"
Mr. Gruber said.

Paddington had a great idea.

He hurried home as fast

as his legs would carry him.

Paddington looked for the picture
Mr. Brown had been painting.
He wondered if this one had
another picture under it, too.

Paddington began to clean.

The boats and blue sky disappeared,

but there was nothing underneath.

The beautiful picture
was now a stormy sea.
Paddington decided
to fix it.

He found some brushes
and an old box of paints.

Then Paddington set to work.

He started to paint
the boats and the lake.
He carefully filled in
the spots he had cleaned.

17

Paddington stepped back

to look at his work.

There was no lake.

There were no boats.

He reached for the paints

and began again.

At dinner that evening,
Paddington was covered
in orange spots.

"I hope you're not getting sick,"
said Mrs. Brown.
She sent him to bed early
just in case.

The next morning,
everyone was happy
to see that Paddington's
spots were gone.

"I have news," said Mr. Brown.

"I have entered a painting contest.

You must all come to the show."

The art show began.
The judges looked
at all the paintings.

Mr. Brown loved painting,

but he had never won a prize.

"This could be it," he said.

The whole family was excited.

The judges announced the winner.

It was Mr. Brown!

But Mr. Brown looked confused.

"This is not my painting!"

said Mr. Brown.

"There must be some mistake."

27

Paddington's painting
on Mr. Brown's canvas
won first prize!

The judges showed Mr. Brown

his name written on the back.

Mr. Brown accepted his prize.
"I think I will donate my prize
to the Home for Retired Bears
in Peru," he said.

Paddington beamed.

"My aunt Lucy will be pleased.

She likes happy endings."

"Don't we all," said Mrs. Bird.